WHEN
GORILLA
GOES
WALKING

WHEN GORILLA GOES WALKING

By Nikki Grimes

Illustrated by Shane Evans

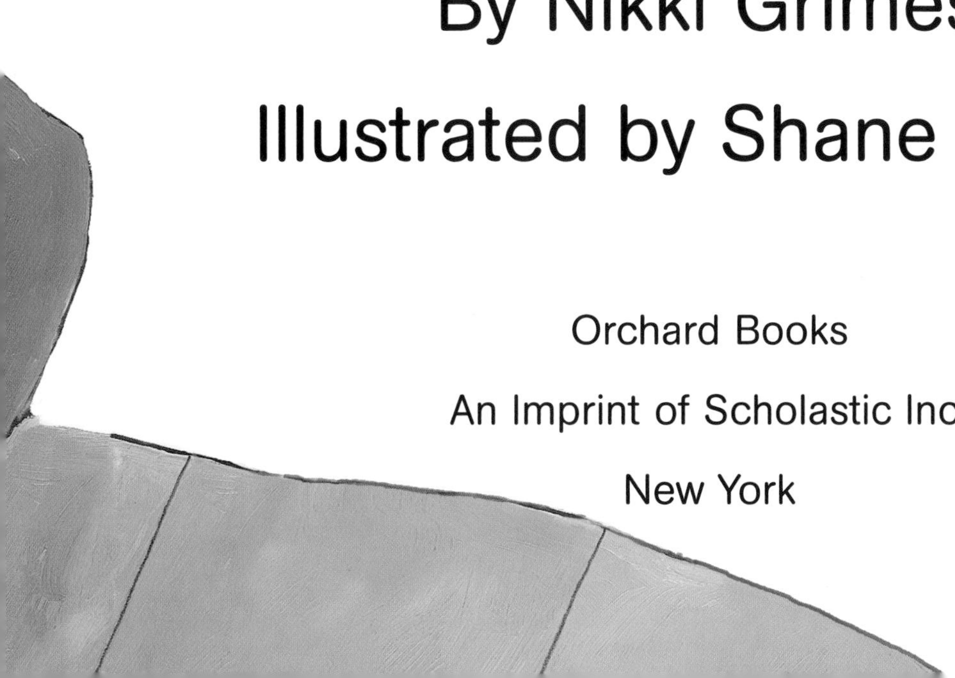

Orchard Books

An Imprint of Scholastic Inc.

New York

CECILIA

Cecilia is my best friend.
Cecilia is my name.
Honey, please don't ask me how
we both were named the same.

Cecilia has three brothers.
I have none at all.
I begged my mother for a pet
and got a cat last fall.

GORILLA

A fierce meow,
a tiger's claws—
Gorilla ain't
no Santa Paws.

She hisses when
a stranger's near.
She chases dogs.
She has no fear.

She has no tail.
She's rain-cloud gray.
I love that cool cat
more each day.

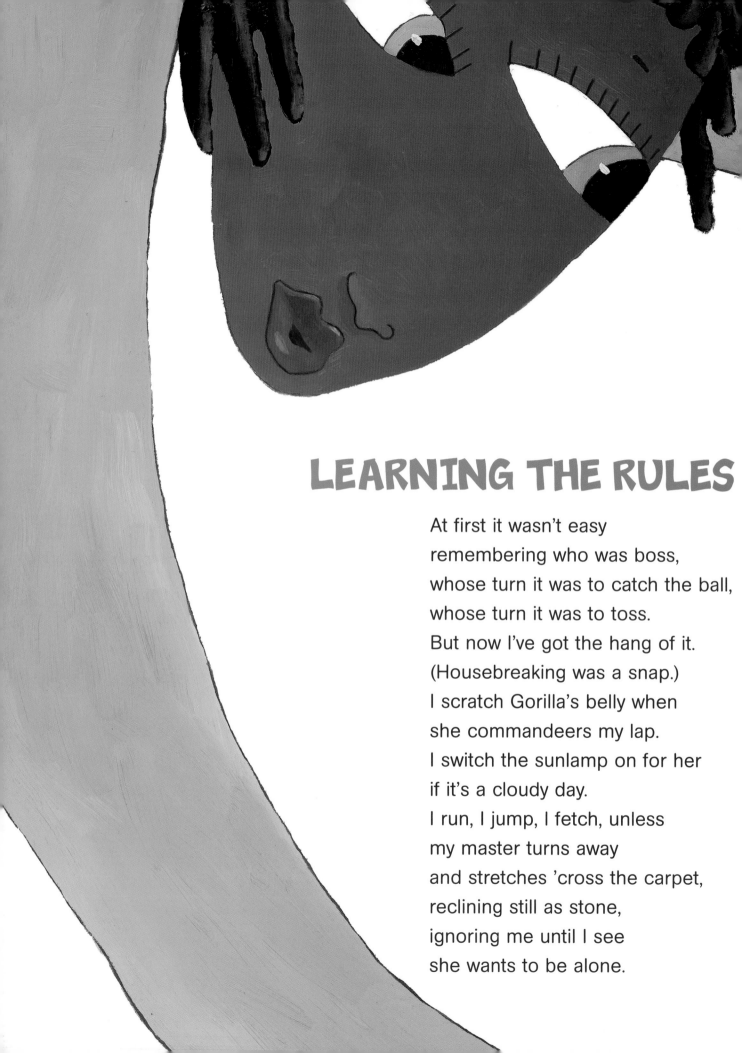

LEARNING THE RULES

At first it wasn't easy
remembering who was boss,
whose turn it was to catch the ball,
whose turn it was to toss.
But now I've got the hang of it.
(Housebreaking was a snap.)
I scratch Gorilla's belly when
she commandeers my lap.
I switch the sunlamp on for her
if it's a cloudy day.
I run, I jump, I fetch, unless
my master turns away
and stretches 'cross the carpet,
reclining still as stone,
ignoring me until I see
she wants to be alone.

PAINTED COLLAR

I bought Gorilla a collar
and slipped it over her head.
It's painted like an African flag.
It's green and black and red.

GORILLA

WHEN GORILLA GOES WALKING

When Gorilla goes walking,
the neighbors laugh and stare
at her tailless rump
and her very proud air.
Her yawn says, "Laugh!
See if I care.
I do not miss the silly thing
'cause it was never there."

SICK DAY

I lay down sick this afternoon.
Gorilla knew and came.
She hopped up on the bed with me,
meowing out my name.

She felt my forehead with her paw.
She listened to my heart.
My every cough and toss and turn
gave her a little start.

Cecilia stopped by to make sure
I wasn't getting worse,
and found me curled up peacefully
beside my feline nurse.

IN THE MIRROR

Gorilla gazes
into a puddle. Does she
know she's beautiful?

BOXING MATCH

The fight was fast.
It wasn't fair.
I should have stopped it.
I was there.
Gorilla flexed her paws,
bared her claws,
and sprang.
Such tragedy!
I couldn't look.
Seven swipes was all it took.

Poor ivy.

TELEPHONE

When the telephone rings
it's a race to see
who will get there first—
Gorilla or me.
She'll leap for the phone
on the kitchen wall
as if she expected
a friendly call
from the fat Siamese
across the street
or the cat next door
in his window seat.
She'll hiss if I say
it's not for her
and walk away
in a huff of fur.

THE DOGHOUSE

Mom says I'm in the doghouse.
Gorilla's in here, too.
Which of us made the bigger mess?
I'll leave that up to you.

I made a finger painting
and left it on the floor.
Gorilla walked across it
and tracked paint to the door.

GAMES

On my birthday I had
a big party
with cheesecake
and strawberry tea.
We played Pin-the-Tail
on Gorilla, and learned
what a rocket
a kitty can be.

BEDTIME

Gorilla has a lovely bed.
Too bad she won't sleep in it.
Instead, she lies beside me
tossing every other minute.
I leave her all the room I can.
It's not enough, it seems.
Gorilla curls so close to me,
I see her in my dreams.

JEALOUS

Gorilla is a jealous cat,
more jealous every day.
I kind of like it, truth be told,
but it gets in the way.

Sometimes she makes me notice her
by pouncing on my book.
She paws every page of my homework
and steals my pen, the crook!

Gorilla makes Cecilia laugh,
wrestling my binder rings.
Each time I pull Gorilla off,
like stubborn me, she clings.

Some days Gorilla scratches me.
"Bad cat! That's it!" I shout.
I chase her to the bedroom door
and coldly shut her out.

Those nights she huddles in the hall
until I climb in bed.
Then she meows outside my door
and butts it with her head.

She purrs out an apology,
her voice so high and thin
she sounds as if her heart will break
if I don't let her in.

"All right, you mangy cat," I growl.
I pad across the floor.
I let her in and scoop her up.
I'm not mad anymore.

LITTLE MISS FUSSY

Gorilla is fussy
about what she eats.
She turns up her nose
at the usual treats.

Forget the canned fish,
and chicken, and liver.
Gorilla likes soul food,
so that's what I give her.

COMFORT

My best friend
packed my heart
and moved away.
Gorilla raised a paw
and pet me.
I think I cried
a dozen times
that day.
Gorilla drank my tears
and let me.

CHASE

Run to the kitchen,
skate 'cross the floor.
Sail by the window,
leap through the door.
Dive from a table,
circle a chair.
Scoot down the hallway,
creep up the stair.
Race past my bedroom
for one more try.
Gorilla will never
catch that fly.

TIME FOR SHOTS

Visits to the vet
always give my pet
the shivers.
I rub her belly
to quiet her fear
and whisper,
"Don't worry!
I'm here."

TOM CAT

His scent brought her
to the window screen.
He was long and lean,
his coat like night,
his paws snow-white.
Gorilla meowed.

It was love
    at first
        sniff.

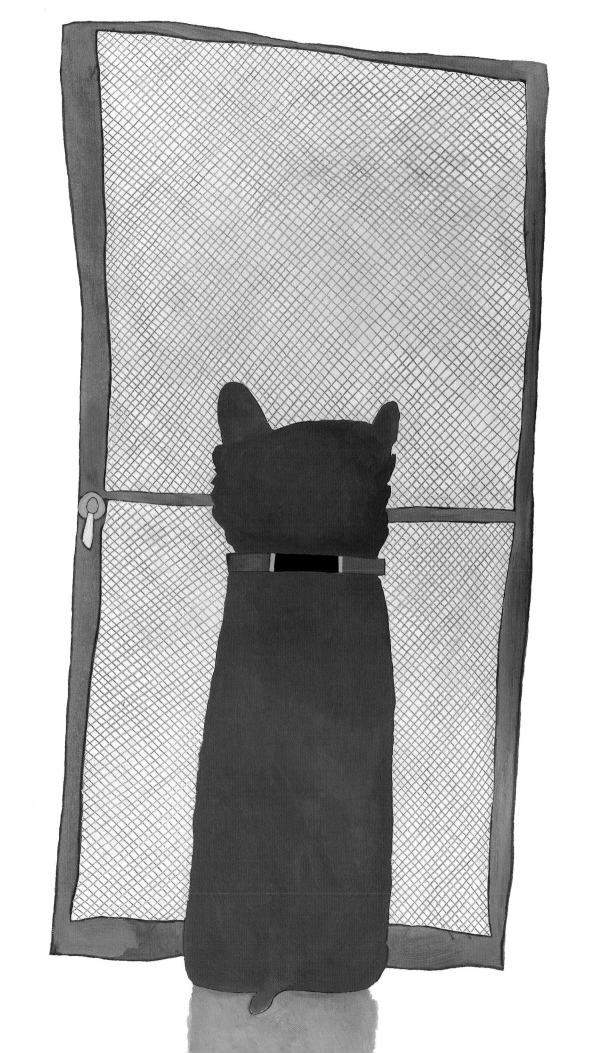

WARNING

Strangers, beware.
If you come to my house,
creep in slowly.
Pretend you're a mouse.
My guard cat is watching.
Touch me and she'll hiss.
Remember this warning
When you see my pet.
I'm Gorilla's human.
Don't ever forget!

**For Aidan Northcutt, his cat Jelly Belly,
and cat lovers everywhere.   -N.G.**

**Thank you, God, Dedicated to "Uncle,"
Linda, Ben, John, and Rio.   -S.W.E.**

Text copyright © 2007 by Nikki Grimes

Illustrations copyright © 2007 by Shane Evans

All rights reserved. Published by Orchard Books, an imprint of Scholastic Inc.,

Publishers since 1920. ORCHARD BOOKS and design are registered trademarks of

Watts Publishing Group, Ltd., used under license. SCHOLASTIC and associated logos

are trademarks and/or registered trademarks of Scholastic Inc.

No part of this publication may be reproduced, stored in a retrieval system, or transmitted

in any form or by any means, electronic, mechanical, photocopying, recording, or otherwise,

without written permission of the publisher. For information regarding permission,

write to Orchard Books, Scholastic Inc., Permissions Department, 557 Broadway, New York, NY 10012.

LIBRARY OF CONGRESS CATALOGING-IN-PUBLICATION DATA

Grimes, Nikki.

When Gorilla Goes Walking / by Nikki Grimes; illustrated by Shane Evans. — 1st ed.   p. cm.

Summary: In this story told in a series of rhyming poems, Gorilla the cat enjoys answering the

telephone, eating soul food, and sharing mischievous adventures with her young owner.

ISBN-13: 978-0-439-31770-2 (alk. paper)

ISBN-10: 0-439-31770-3

[1. Cats—Fiction. 2. African Americans—Fiction. 3. Stories in rhyme.] I. Evans, Shane, ill.

II. Title. PZ8.3.G8875Wh 2007 [E]—dc22 2006017194

Printed in Singapore   46   Reinforced Binding for Library Use

The art was created using Alkyd paints.

The text type was set in AG Rounded Regular, and display type were set in AG Old Face Bold.

Book design by Marijka Kostiw